The Happy Husband's Handbook

by
Sly Fleming

Bloomington, IN  Milton Keynes, UK

authorHOUSE™

AuthorHouse™
1663 Liberty Drive, Suite 200
Bloomington, IN 47403
www.authorhouse.com
Phone: 1-800-839-8640

AuthorHouse™ UK Ltd.
500 Avebury Boulevard
Central Milton Keynes, MK9 2BE
www.authorhouse.co.uk
Phone: 08001974150

This book is a work of non-fiction. Unless otherwise noted, the author and the publisher make no explicit guarantees as to the accuracy of the information contained in this book and in some cases, names of people and places have been altered to protect their privacy.

First published by AuthorHouse 3/14/2006

ISBN: 1-4259-2078-0 (sc)

Printed in the United States of America
Bloomington, Indiana

This book is printed on acid-free paper.

Acknowledgements

I will start, as I always do, by giving honor to my Father in Heaven and thanking Him for the wisdom and guidance he has given me. I was blessed to hold the pen that He anointed, and I pray that same anointing flows to you for understanding.

I acknowledge my helpmeet and gift from God, my wife, and my two God-given prophets, Isaiah and Samuel.

I'd like to thank my pastor and church family at Rainbow Family Christian Center (www.rainbowfamilychristian.org) and give special recognition to the church of my youth, Covenant United Presbyterian Church. I also want to send love to the place of my youth, Fishertown, North Carolina, and all those Fishertonians who are still around. I owe a lot of you many things and I keep all of you in my prayers, especially those who have experienced great lost. To my close cousin Marcus, welcome back--glad to have you home. To my father and mother, thanks for your guidance and love. To all my grandparents it has been nothing but a pure blessing having you in my life. To my in-laws, I don't believe I should have it this good, because your love has been constant and unconditional. To all my brothers and sisters (including my brothers-in-law) life is good because I have you.

I'd also like to honor my extended family members: the Flemings of New Jersey, the Flemings of North Carolina, the Cannon's of North Carolina, the Lytle's of North Carolina, the Lytle's of Pennsylvania, the Cannons of California, the Partee's of Washington, DC, the Latimer's of New Jersey and Maryland,, The Whites of North Carolina, the

Stockton's of North Carolina, the Mukasa-Magoye family, and my enormous Buganda family. To Levi and Bryant, I send love and thanks to both of your families, because they're also my family.

Finally, to the individuals who helped me with my first book, thank you. Special thanks to Grace Beauty Salon, Dr. Eugene Williams, Audrey Chapman, Marsha Summers, Connie at Barnes and Nobles Bowie, Kini and my special staff member from Walden Books in Forestville, Redeemer Child Care Center. To all my fellow authors, we've labored together, so don't give up the faith. To all the churches and groups that invited me to speak, I say thank you. Thanks also to my editors Laura Jackson from LCJ Communications and Esther from Infocusva, LLC. Without you, this wouldn't be possible. Last, but not least, I thank you, the reader, for buying the book, reading it and telling others about it. No man is an island, so if I stand tall it's because I stand on the shoulders of others.

Contents

Introduction

How many times have you heard the expression, ball and chain, or maybe you heard a groom being referred to as a dead man walking. In most situations the night before a marriage, some one always tell the groom, you better enjoy this because this is your last night of freedom, most of the time it is the single guy or an unhappy marriage one. How many times have you wondered if there are truly happy husbands out there among you in society? The answer is there are. How many times have you heard, things are going to change after you get married, or she will change, or it could be you that change? This book is here to show you that change is not always a bad thing; you just have to know how to change.

If you are married, have you ever heard the phrase or the advice, if you can make it the first couple of years your marriage will be fine: as if there is an magical cruise control that you hit and coast along. Chances are that some change took place. The reason of the pain associated with change has nothing to do with marriage, it deals with the fact that you have two individuals blending two lives into one. Trust me, it is not easy, but always worth it if it is done right.

Have you ever wondered how can a woman that you love so much, get you so mad or vice-versa? Have you ever look at your relationship as a heavy weight fight versus the loving environment you used to see on "Leave it to Beaver?" Many people search for years for an owner's manual for marriage, so they could just find some direction on how to be a Happy Husband. In this book we will give you some ideas on how to become a Happy Husband. This book breaks down 10 key elements in the beginning of your relationship and marriage that can lead to becoming a Happy Husband. This book also gives important to do's and take away's from each chapter, while following them up with meaningful scripture readings. This book is written in the likeness of a manual in order to spark action and implementation of change to approach a long life for you and a better bond with your spouse.

Because people are different, all or maybe none of the suggestions in this book may work for you. I am a strong believer that you will be able to pull something from this book to help you to walk in your path to becoming a happier husband. Remember that this process will not be an overnight event, but neither was your proposal to your wife. However, you deserve a chance to make your situation better, even if it is just a little bit better. We all must face the fact that this book might not be for everyone, you could be that one person where everything is perfect and there is no room for improvement and if that is you; you are an outstanding person or a person locked in denial, you make the call. But don't make this call in front of your wife, your not ready for that conversation right now. But for the rest of you please enjoy, mold, and create this book in your own lives and situations.

I have a feeling that some of you will like this book; and some of you will not. Some of you will make your relationships better and some will not attempt it. But I believe you all deserve the chance to make your marriage the best you can. So I'll finish by saying enjoy this book and make it your own and if it indeed helps you, tell a friend and start a trend of Happy Husbands.

CHAPTER 1

STANDING IN THE G.A.P.

So you want to be the head of the house, the big fish, the big man on campus, the say all and be all? You want to snap your fingers and have all your desires come into existence? You want life to be so good that "obey" becomes your wife's middle name?

Wake up and stop dreaming! Those days of acting like a caveman to get your wife to submit have long gone. Plus, I've seen a few cavewomen and, no disrespect, but they're not my type. But don't be discouraged, my brother. We as men do have a duty to be the head of our households, but it's extremely difficult if God isn't the head of your life.

To be a good leader or head of the house, you must be a great follower. How else can we lead while we're also keeping a job, paying bills, participating in church, trying to stay in physical shape, and building a life with a wife and maybe some kids? We don't have time to redesign and create a new socially viable way of living. And can you imagine convincing the world that your way is right? You have a hard enough time at home with the people who love you. Why try to reinvent the wheel?

Let me tell you a secret: You won't have to coach or tell your wife to support and respect you if she knows you're worth following. If you're equally yoked with your mate, you must stand in the G.A.P. to have a fulfilling marriage. The letters G.A.P. stands for God-Appointed Place.

How many times have you heard your significant other make a "genie comment?" For example, "I wish you would do this," or "I wish you wouldn't do that?" Even if she had used up her three wishes a long time ago, the requests keep coming. The reason your spouse continues to wish is because she doesn't see how your vision lines up with God, or you're not always in line with that vision. In other words, you're not in your God-Appointed Place.

What's this appointed place? Does it come with a cup of coffee or maybe two tickets to the Super Bowl? Let's break down the meaning of these words and figure out how we can get to this location.

God: God is the Supreme One, the creator of heaven and earth, man and woman. God said that it wasn't good for man to be alone. He made man from the dust of the ground and gave us life (see Gen. 2:7). He then put man in a deep sleep to remove one of his ribs to make woman (Gen. 2:21-22). This means that woman belongs to man, and man is incomplete without woman.

When God made man, he made him in His own image-- and this was before He made woman. Once you're married, you and your spouse began a process of becoming one in the image of God.

The key to this oneness is that man must remain focused on God for his instructions, and woman must remain focused on man so that their steps might be ordered by God. Man was made to be the head of this chain of command. However, just like during times of war, if the leader isn't in place, the orders will go to the next in line. If you've been missing in action from your God-Appointed Place, it will take time to restore order. Perhaps you've been wondering why the natives haven't been impressed by your annual Easter or Christmas pilgrimage to the local church. They also weren't moved when you declared yourself the spiritual leader of your home, sat on your throne in front of the playoff game, and informed your wife that she should honor your godly attitude by making you a sandwich.

Truly allowing God to be the head of your life requires gradual, continual change, so putting a deadline on her reaction will only produce disappointment. To be a good leader, you must stay focused on the goal without leaving the troops behind. So stay focused on God for revelation, not her, because she's looking to you for direction.

Appointed: God made you for a specific duty and you're appointed and anointed for that task. It doesn't matter if you can run faster than a speeding bullet or jump a tall building in a single bound. You are **not** operating at 100 percent efficiency until you're appointed and anointed.

The King James Version of the Bible states, "But seek ye first the kingdom of God, and His righteousness; and all these things shall be added unto you (Matt. 6:33)." In other words, God promises that if you focus on Him, He'll handle the rest.

When you walk in His purpose and anointing, you'll find favor and peace.

Place: This is where God would have you to be—not necessarily where you want to be. God will place you--you will not place God. I think I need to say that again. God will put you in the places in life that He has for you.

After high school, for example, I knew I had choices to make: go to work, go to the service, or go to college. I was now a man, and I had to leave my father's house. I wanted to go to college, but I needed to select a major. When I went to my guidance counselor for help, he told me to take a job in the local textile mill. He wasn't talking my language. Because I thought that all adults would give me poor advice, I kept them out of my decision-making process--and I didn't pray either.

My grand epiphany was to approach this the logical way: I picked up *Fortune* magazine and looked at which profession was making the most money at the time. Right up top was a category called engineering. I knew I wanted to have money and wear a suit to work, so with this foundation I used the weeding-out technique.

Because I couldn't draw, I knew I had no chance at architectural engineering. Next was civil engineering-- making bridges and roads. Nope, too much time out in the sun, plus I can't swim well enough to spend time in the middle of a body of water on an unfinished bridge. Then there was mechanical engineering, which didn't fit my criteria because I didn't want to mess with air ducts and grease. Industrial engineering was close, but these engineers had to travel from plant to plant firing people, a term they called "rightsizing." I just didn't want to be the bearer of bad news. When I thought of nuclear engineering, all I could imagine was glowing in the dark. And at that time, computer engineering was still just a science.

So by process of elimination, I chose electrical engineering. After all, in all the old movies these guys had on suits when they took off their lab coats. Friends and family members tried to tell me that engineering wasn't for me. Instead of hearing what they were saying, I let my pride tell me that they didn't believe in me. So I pushed myself through the engineering program and got a job making a good salary. I wore a suit, but I wasn't happy. Several years later I went back to school for a master's in business.

Even though I was good at engineering, it wasn't my place. I might have succeeded for a season or two, but not for much longer. You might be in a situation, a group, or a physical location where you find yourself without favor because it's not your place. How many self-proclaimed leaders and saviors do we know, who have good intentions but just can't seem to get it together? Are they operating in His favor at 100 percent efficiency? Are you?

TAKE AWAY'S

1. Check the place where you're standing.

2. Make sure God is leading you. Don't try to take the lead using your finite wisdom.

3. Focus on God and not the results—you'll succeed with time.

4. Lead your wife. Don't push or pull her.

5. Make it evident that God is the head of your life.

_TO DO's_

1. Write down the things you do well in life and in your relationship. Ask yourself how you use these talents in service to God.

2. Make time to read your Bible and pray so that you can receive instruction from God.

3. Continue to seek His wisdom in all that you do.

4. Pray and read the Word of God with your wife.

5. Find your God-Appointed Place.

SCRIPTURE READINGS

1. I will instruct thee and teach thee in the way
    which thou shalt go: I will guide thee with
    mine eye.   *Psalm 32:8*

2. In all thy ways acknowledge Him, and He
    shall direct thy paths.   *Proverbs 3:6*

3. The steps of a good man are ordered by the
    Lord: and he delighteth in his way.
    Psalm 37:23

4. A man's heart deviseth his way: but the Lord
    directeth his steps. *Proverbs 16:9*

5. For his God doth instruct him to discretion,
    and doth teach him.   *Isaiah 28:26*

CHAPTER 2

KNOW THAT YOU'RE DIFFERENT

For many years, we've been told that men and women are as different as the east is from the west. We even have books that say we're from different planets. Many times, individuals look at these differences as obstacles in their relationship--problems to overcome. For them, difference causes disconnection.

Let's look at it from another prospective. God made man and He said that it was not good for man to be alone. Why would He make woman, the ultimate helpmeet, the same as man? What would be the benefit? If man and woman were the same, they would double their strength-- and their weaknesses. Things that would excite them would really excite them, but things that depressed them would really depress them. They'd be in an ongoing battle to find balance.

Normally the man is a machine of logic and reaction, whereas the woman is a blossoming flower of emotion and precognitive thought. Remember I said normally, because sometimes it's vice-versa. In either case, just because something is different doesn't mean it's broken. Unfortunately, some of us enter into a relationship thinking that we can change our mates. That's not going to happen. The only person you can change is yourself.

A friend once shared this idea with me: Once people tell you who they are, believe them. Suppose you met your wife in a club, and she was half-dressed and bouncing from guy to guy. Don't believe that just because she has your ring on her finger, all of her urges will disappear into the magic cloud of forgetfulness. She might not change just because you've forbidden her ever to go to a club again. The only thing you can do is be holy and allow God to work on her, because your work permit doesn't cover the reconstruction of a mate.

Men and women are different--and it's a blessing. Will we as men ever completely understand women? Maybe one day we will, but it won't be in your lifetime or mine. But we can still make our relationships work. We men need to watch our wives, understand how to read their body language, and learn their tendencies. **Caution:** I'm not telling you to go around stalking your wife, following her around the house with a notepad as if she's a science project. Just realize that a closed, locked door might mean she wants some time alone, so give her some respect.

Typically, men are very simple creatures, whereas women are complex. Understanding your wife will require a lifetime of committed effort. The more you commit, and the longer you're together, the better the relationship or the more you understand?

So find out things that she likes, the things she'd like you to do for her, and the things she likes to do for you. Trust me, she'll give you signs. Our job is to recognize and decode them. Prioritize the things she likes and try to implement them into your schedule without her asking you to do so. If she likes to do things for you, find a way to let her, even if it makes you look inadequate. Early in my marriage, my wife wanted to iron and press all my shirts. I felt that I could do them and didn't want her to feel that she had to be my maid. But this was an expression of love from her and a way for her to feel that she was making my day better.

Also earlier in my marriage, I would find myself trying to buy my wife the finer things in life, just to show my wife how much I cared. She would just smile and say, "I don't need these things to know you love me." Needless to say, this wasn't the response I wanted. I remember back to one Thursday during the spring, I decided to stay home and do some spring cleaning instead of going on a golf outing. I put some music on, and I had so much fun that I didn't even think of it as cleaning. The house was spotless, and I put a lovely meal on the table for my wife, who'd been working all day. That was the No. 1 thing that she wanted me to do for her, and my effort brought tears of joy and a response I couldn't imagine. I'd been delivering pretty, red *apples* and all she wanted was one semi-sweet *orange*.

Once you find a way to make your wife cry tears of joy, you're on the path to great things (putting onions in her pillow at night doesn't count). However, if you find yourself unable to catch on to your wife's subtle hints, just remember: When all else fails, just ask. Women believe we're simple and direct, so it's OK to use this perception to our advantage.

Warning: In the case of pregnancy, just pray, hang on, and don't answer any questions. She knows the answer and you don't and she wants to hear you say it, lets just say the bravest of men have crashed and fallen to their own egos during this time. The whole moral of this chapter is to let you know that men and women are different, don't try to change it, embrace it.

Remember in a marriage you will have your up days as well as your down days. You are two individuals who have decided to blend your lives into one. This is not an easy thing to do and after the honeymoon it is only the beginning. For the most part you have learned to live as a self sufficient individual, having things done your way or the highway. Now you are sharing every detail of your life with your spouse, which bring a new meaning to the phrase easier said than done.

Let's focus on the bad days, because these are the days where you will need that extra little strength. Because when life happens, and you and your love one is expressing every emotion except for extreme happiness. And it seems life has got you over a barrel and no one understands or cares for you, this is the time when it is easy to speak out of hate and not love, don't let that be you. Always speak out of love and when you can not speak in love, just be silent and allow yourself the opportunity to regain focus on what is important. When emotions are high, take time to focus on your friendship and allow your marriage a chance to breathe. Do something that presents you and your wife the opportunity to take you mind off of the source of your indignation. But before you leave on a mission destine for fun and acting in a care free manner, establish a time and a place, where you two will sit down and effectively discuss the problem and search together for a solution.

TAKE AWAY'S

1. Men and women are different.

2. Opposites normally attract and make each other stronger.

3. You can't change your spouse.

4. It's OK to be simple and direct (play dumb).

5. During pregnancy, all bets are off. Just pray and speak as little as possible.

_TO DO's_

1. Make a list of both of your strengths, weaknesses, opportunities, and threats for yourself to be referred to by yourself. DO NOT show your spouse a list of her weaknesses as a score card or a look what I am good at and you are not approach.

2. Do things without being asked.

3. Look for signals from your wife to begin a different level of communicating.

4. Make a lifetime commitment to getting to know your wife.

5. Learn to lean on one another so together you'll be stronger than either of you could be alone.

SCRIPTURE READINGS

1. God created man in His own image, in the image of God created He him; male and female created He them. *Genesis 1:27*

2. The Lord God formed man of the dust of the ground, and breathed into his nostrils the breath of life; and the man became a living soul. *Genesis 2:7*

3. The LORD God said, it is not good that the man should be alone; I will make him an help meet for him. *Genesis 2:18*

4. So the Lord God caused the man to fall into a deep sleep, and while he was sleeping, He took one of the man's ribs and closed up the place with flesh. Then the LORD God made a woman from the rib, he had taken out of the man, and he brought her to the man. *Genesis 2: 21-22*

5. The man said, "This is now bone of my bones, and flesh of my flesh; she shall be called woman for she was taken out of man. For this reason a man will leave his father and mother and be

united to his wife, and they will become one flesh.   *Genesis 2:23-24*

6. For the Husband is the head of the wife as Christ is the head of the church, his body, of which he is the Savior.   *Ephesians 5:23*

CHAPTER 3

WIN THE WAR
NOT EVERY BATTLE

Most women think ahead and stay in touch with their emotions along the way. Thank God for that--could you imagine a world without a mother's instinct--or if men had babies? On the other hand, most men are reactive and logical, which comes in handy as they're the protectors of their families. But this difference puts men at a disadvantage during an argument.

When your wife wakes you up at 2:30 a.m. in the morning to talk or finish a conversation you had a few days ago, or she stands between you and the fourth quarter of the playoff game you've been watching for the past hour and a half (I hope you have Tivo), just remember that, in this situation, you're outgunned. She's played this conversation over and over in her mind before she even approached you. Some man out there has been held hostage in a corner for approximately 30 minutes listening to his wife tell him that he doesn't listen, and his only response is, "I am listening," which only infuriates his wife even more. He forgot that men are reactionary, and in her mind she knew he was going to say he is listening, which only added fuel to the fire.

Regardless of the problem, you need time to think it out, so you need to create a strategy or for the lack of a better term an exit plan to allow to get back in her good graces while at the same time creating an atmosphere of peace. Here's a two-word phrase that in more times than not will attend to the problem without engaging in a losing argument. This phrase has saved men of all ages in all countries for centuries. The simple but powerful phrase that has captured the hearts of women is, "Yes, dear." Now, once you say "Yes, dear," you must be quiet. Don't engage—simply stop talking, let her have the last word, and re-group. By the way, did I say stop talking? After all, it takes two to argue.

During her monologue, think of a happy place--maybe the beach or the golf course, or the time when you first fell in love and married her. It can be your very own little secret. Not engaging is the key to a long, happy life. Why do you think the average woman lives longer than a man? Because the average man engages in arguments so he can declare himself the leader of the domain. A real leader, however, doesn't have to tell anyone that he's the leader. The men who don't engage and compete in something they weren't designed for: live to a ripe old age.

The words "Yes, dear" will give your wife something unexpected, which confirms that you're listening. It's hard to argue when you both are standing on the same side looking at the problem. Plus, you reduce the time of heated discussion or arguing considerably. **Caution:** Please listen to what she's saying before you go throwing out the words "Yes, dear" as a surrender plea, because this could have an adverse response. For instance, if she asks, "Do you think I'm getting fat and angry in my old age?", "Yes, dear" wouldn't work.

You might be saying, "This will never work on my wife. She was born to argue. Conflict is her national pastime. She needs strife in my life for breakfast." During times like these, you should go straight to the ultimate source, the Bible. Just gently say, "**Yes, dear**, I see there's a problem. Let's go to the Bible together to see what **instruction God** has for us in this situation and then we can **pray over it**." I don't know about your situation, but it's almost impossible for her to stay mad when you have Jesus as your mediator. Don't use this option lightly, as in, "If you don't make me a sandwich, we're going to have to see what the Bible says about a wife not feeding her husband." If you use this tactic as a joke, it will become one.

Sometimes you just need to go up to your spouse and give her a gentle, meaningful hug while whispering in her ear, "I had no idea you felt that way. I'll truly work on being the husband you need me to be, but I'm going to need your help, your patience, and your prayers. Can I depend on you as my helpmeet?" The whole object isn't to avoid disagreements but to not engage in arguments.

You can avoid most arguments just by paying attention. For instance, if you're in front of an important game and your wife says she needs to talk, don't brush her off until after the game. This will send the message that the game is more important to you than she is and, trust me, she'll interrupt more games. So in order to prevent this argument (sounds like a Tivo moment) let her know how much this game means to you but how much more she means to you. Take that time to talk to your wife, but also tape the game. This mere action of stopping something that's important to you will add an abundance of happiness to her and a new sense of peace when watching future games. She won't interrupt your game--and she won't let anyone else bother you either because she no longer feels threatened by the time you spend in front of the TV.

You also can avoid frequent fights by choosing your battles wisely. Remember the story of the boy who cried wolf? Do you want to be like him? If you argue in every situation, how will your spouse knows what really matters? Everything doesn't have to be a battle, and you don't have to bring out the big guns for every discussion. I'm not saying lose your backbone--it's harder to walk away from a fight than it is to engage in one--but you're a leader, and as leader you should focus on the greater good, not your own personal ego. Choosing your battles might require some perceived personal sacrifice at first, but it will pay off in the grand scheme of things.

Finally, keep these do's and don'ts in mind:

1. Never, ever, ever, engage in an argument during times of unbalanced emotions, such as pregnancy.

2. Never engage in a public argument, because pride will becomes part of the argument. Further, don't engage in arguments in front of friends, family, or colleagues.

3. Keep your hands to yourself. You want to remain loving and caring at all times.

4. Never forget or take your eye off of the reason that you two are together.

5. Being humble is not being week, matter of fact it takes more strength to do so.

TAKE AWAY'S

1. Emotions drive most women. Logic drives most men.

2. Don't engage in a fruitless argument.

3. Stay focused on the greater good which is your marriage.

4. Use the Bible and prayer to diffuse heated situations by allowing you both to focus on biblical law versus your own feelings.

5. Remember the words, "Yes, dear" and use them wisely.

TO DO's

1. Choose your battles wisely.

2. The louder and angrier she becomes the quieter and calmer you need to be.

3. Always remember why you love her. (If necessary, write it down, use pictures, and so on.)

4. Put your wife's needs above your own.

5. Show your wife respect by keeping your problems out of the public.

SCRIPTURE READINGS

1. Whosoever therefore shall humble himself as this little child, the same is greatest in the kingdom of heaven.   *Matthew 18:4*

2. Better it is to be of humble spirit with the lowly, than to divide the spoil with the proud. *Proverbs 16: 19*

3. Behold, thou desirest truth in the inward parts: and in the hidden part thou shalt make me to know wisdom.   *Psalm 51:6*

4. A soft answer turneth away wrath: but grievous words stir up anger.   *Proverbs 15:1*

5. With the ancient is wisdom; and in length of days understanding. With him is wisdom and strength, he hath counsel and understanding. *Job 12: 12-13*

CHAPTER 4
LISTEN

Listening is probably one of the most important things you'll ever need to know how to do. However, it's one of the hardest things to master, because men and women speak different languages and their interests aren't always the same.

Have you ever wondered why you catch yourself drifting off from a conversation sometimes? Your wife starts telling you about a big sale she encountered at the mall, and you find yourself thinking about something that has no connection at all, like whatever happened to the guy who played Keith on the TV show "*Good Times*"? You drift back right before she asks you a question that pertains to something you missed during the conversation. So you do what most men do at this moment: they grunt, moan, or mumble, "You don't say?"

You're not sick or fading away because you're bored or don't care about the things that interest your wife. You're just different. Have you ever found yourself falling asleep in a movie that your wife said was a moving and meaningful film, full of emotional character, and all you could remember is that the movie had no action or suspense? The same thing happens to her when you talk sports, play golf, go fishing, or want to watch a very important game. So, fellas, pay close attention because I'm going to give you some important keys to listening to your wife.

1. Make good eye contact. This lets your wife know that she has your undivided attention and that her words truly matter. If the conversation you're having with your wife makes it hard to look her in the eye, focus on her lips, nose, or maybe her forehead, but look attentive. If she's

not appealing at that time--maybe because of tears and running makeup--just remember how lovely she really is and how she make you feel on the good days.

2. Set the proper mood for conversation by turning off all distractions. This sends the message that nothing is more important to you than communicating with her. This will also allow both of you to talk in a calm, soft tone.

3. Set a time to talk so that you're not worried about missing a prior engagement. Planning time to talk also helps both sides settle emotions and think about what they want to say.

4. Listen to the meaning of the words she's saying, not just the sound. It won't hurt to remember a couple of key points, because most women remember entire conversations, especially if they consider the discussions important. She might recall and take advantage of this information at a later time in your marriage, so make sure you remember what you said as well. (Another reason why "Yes, dear" is so perfect.) Further, she might ask questions while talking to you just to check and see if you're still listening.

5. Be quick to listen and slow to speak. You'll have your chance to speak, but select your words carefully. A wrong word could start a chain of events that would make a day of surgery seem pleasant. If during the conversation you don't know what to say, put your hands in the praying mode, place them under your chin, very slightly shake you head in acknowledgement and say, "I had no idea." Or you can fall back on the faithful "Yes, dear," especially if you messed up.

6. Most men focus through physical contact, so try to find a way to implement it into your conversation. Maybe you can hold her hand and walk through the park or sit her on your lap and comb or play with her hair. Sometimes she'll return the favor by massaging your shoulders. Think about these things carefully beforehand, however. If she's extremely mad at you, for instance, you might not want to play in her hair. And make sure you remember that you're supposed to be talking. If you start looking for ways to gain affection, you'll take away's from all the things you've done. <might want to clarify this.>

7. Don't be too afraid or proud to ask your wife for clarification. Don't blindly agree to terms and changes. Ask for details or an example. You'll better understand what she's talking

about and her words will become more real to you.

8. If your wife begins to cry, don't shut her down or try to suppress her emotions. And this isn't the time to go in for the kill shot. Just give her time to get herself together and let her know that you're there for her.

9. Always end your conversations with a hug and a kiss, and always tell your wife that you love her no matter how you might feel about her at that time. Remember, love is a choice. It's easy to say "I love you" when things are going well, but it takes love to say those words during difficult and trying times. Saying those three little words after a difficult conversation will ease awkward feelings and end the discussion on positive note.

10. To improve overall communication with your spouse, learn your wife's body language. Some women might not be as straight forward as men, so when we ask a simple question we get lost in the response, or we take a word literally when we shouldn't. Master the art of reading between the lines. Understand her eyes, the way she stands, the sound of her voice, her movements, her silence, and more. She's communicating to you in more ways than just verbally.

11. Consider keeping a journal for your eyes only. I know most men don't have journals, but we should. Remember all the information you used to keep in your little black book? Now, instead of keeping a few important notes on a few different people, you have a viable source of information for yourself on your wife. If your goal is to make your marriage better you have to study and keep notes in your journal. You'll create a perfect playbook for your marriage. Also, write the things that you and your wife are praying for, add a date, and note the outcome. Your journal will come to your rescue time and time again.

TAKE AWAY'S

1. Listening is vital.

2. Learn to listen, not just hear.

3. Be quick to listen and slow to speak.

4. Most women remember everything said during a conversation.

5. Don't try to change her.

TO DO's

1. Make good eye contact and listen.

2. Keep a journal

3. Once a month make your wife feel as if she's the only one in the world that matters.

4. If you don't understand ask for clarification.

SCRIPTURE READINGS

1. He that answereth a matter before he heareth it, it is folly and shame unto him. *Proverbs 18:13*

2. A wise man will hear, and will increase learning; and a man of understanding shall attain unto wise counsels. *Proverbs 1:5*

3. My dear brothers, take note of this: Everyone should be quick to listen, slow to speak and slow to become angry... *James 1:19*

4. When words are many, sin is not absent, but he who holds his tongue is wise. *Proverbs 10:19*

5. Guard your steps when you go to the house of God. Go near to listen rather than to offer the sacrifice of fools, who do not know that they do wrong. Do not be quick with your mouth, do not be hasty in your heart to utter anything before God. God is in heaven and you are on earth, so let your words be few. *Ecclesiastes 5:1-2*

CHAPTER 5

DON'T GO TO BED ANGRY

Have you ever wondered why people say, "Never go to bed mad," or "Never let the sun go down on your anger"? You can find one reason for these phrases in another truism: "Tomorrow is not promised to you." In my book *30 Days of Love,* I wrote a poem entitled *Love Unreturned* that talks about this matter. How would you feel if the person you loved didn't wake up the next morning, and your lifetime of love ended in anger or an argument? Death is too final, and you shouldn't allow this to happen to you and your wife.

A huge explosion of an argument makes it easy to detect anger in your spouse before you go to bed, but what about silent resentment? Out of all the types of anger, this is the one that's the most threatening to your marriage. If you or your spouse harbors silent resentment, it will grow and unexpectedly erupt when you both least expect it.

Have you ever become lost while driving, and before you have a chance to speak; you heard that you never ask for directions, and you knew that you didn't know where you were going in the first place? Before long the conversation goes from driving, to how you never cook, you never clean, and you never listen. And it doesn't stop there. Next you're hearing comments about your family and friends; clearly some emotion has built up over time and has finally exploded.

One way to keep this mountain from erupting on you at any given time is to release pressure daily. Agree with your wife to take at least 15 minutes each night before bed to talk and clear the air. You'll rid yourselves of any hidden resentment and start with a clean slate every morning-- which comes in handy since we all need plenty of space for mistakes. When you eliminate hidden resentments and issues, the words "Good morning" will have more meaning and sincerity.

Of course, you can't resolve some discussions in a 15-minute time frame, so you and your wife might need to agree to discuss the problem in greater detail later. You don't have to go to bed happy, just not angry. Set the discussion aside, and remember to keep her first no matter how tired you might be. Trust me, your sleep will be more enjoyable if it's not accompanied by accidental bumps and bruises throughout the night. I can't say it enough: Stay focused on what's important. Would you rather love or fight with the ones you love? After all is said and done, kiss your wife, tell her you love her, pray with her, and then say good night.

TAKE AWAY'S

1. Life is short. Don't let angry words be the last ones you ever say to your wife.

2. Subtle anger is a real threat.

3. To make your marriage work, make a commitment to talk with your spouse at least 15 minutes every night.

4. It's OK not to change the world in one night but have hope for tomorrow and move forward.

_TO DO's_

1. Spend time talking to your wife before bed.

2. Pray together before bed.

3. Tell your wife you love her before bed.

4. Don't discount the degree of your wife's anger.

5. Keep your wife's needs first before going to sleep, even if that means you miss a few minutes of sleep.

SCRIPTURE READINGS

1. The Lord is gracious, and full of compassion; slow to anger, and of great mercy.
    Psalm 145:8

2. Be not hasty in thy spirit to be angry: for anger resteth in the bosom of fools.   *Ecclesiastes 7:9*

3. It is better to dwell in the wilderness, than with a contentious and an angry woman.
    Proverbs 21:19

4. He that is soon angry dealeth foolishly ….
    Proverbs 14:17

5. A wrathful man stirreth up strife: but he that is slow to anger appeaseth strife.   *Proverbs 15:18*

CHAPTER 6

JUST SAY NO!!!

What were you looking for in a woman before you met your wife? Do you remember the traits that attracted you to her and how your actions were affected by those traits? Just because you're a married man now doesn't mean that you're no longer attracted to those things. What attracted you as a single man will still find its way into your vision and appeal to you as a married man.

Don't think a band of platinum or gold can fend off all the types of women that attracted you earlier in your life. Most times, just the opposite happens. You've now become what most women want--a man of confidence and stability--but you have a lot more to lose. This is hard to face if you're not ready because this is a time that a lot of men dreamed of, when they're the wanted man, the hunk, the eye candy that you can see but not touch. This is the time when women might come up to you and make an offer.

However, this is the time when you say no--no to allowing another woman into your private life and no to allowing another woman to know your innermost secrets. Refuse to put yourself in a position of compromise that will require you to explain your actions to your wife, family, friends, and society.

Whether you're at work, church, or just on the street, you must remain focused on the responsibilities you have as a husband and the promises and duties you're obligated to keep.

It's not easy to say no to the woman of your so-called dreams. Just remember the devil comes to kill, steal, and destroy--and the worst part is that he knows how to tempt you but the ultimate choice is yours. The woman who offers an opportunity might be beautiful, but what will it cost you? Never forget there are lots of exits on the highway of unfaithfulness, and it's up to you to take the exit. It won't be easy-- the enemy will make sure she has all the traits your wife doesn't. If you're not careful, you'll find yourself believing that the grass is greener on the other side of the fence. I'm here to tell you your grass can be just as green or greener if you take the time to care for and nurture what you already have and it is amazing how green the grass can be at home.

Any time you feel you're about to wind up in a situation that's detrimental to your marriage, spend more time in the Word and with your wife. You only have one chance to be a faithful husband, because once you mess up and she finds out about your unfaithfulness, things will never be exactly the same.

To be a faithful husband you must examine yourself honestly. For starters, use this list to identify your strengths, weaknesses, opportunities, and threats: This is a common business analysis known as the S.W.O.T. analysis but it can work in your personal life.

1. **Strengths**: What strengths and traits can you use to defend yourself against a potential seductress? For instance, you might have a strong character or sense of honor that prevents you from hurting your wife or going back on a promise. It might be your love for your wife or the fact that you want your children's respect. Could it be your Bible and desire to please God? Whatever your weapon might be, find and use it to stay on course.

2. **Weaknesses:** Are you the guy who can't say no to a beautiful woman? Has your wife warned that a certain woman wants you, and you believe the woman is just being nice? Knowing your weakness can prevent you from finding yourself in a dangerous situation. In some cases, for example, you might have to stay in public places and avoid being alone with certain women.

3. **Opportunities**: Your opportunity is your wife and your time to grow with her. Tell your wife your needs and how important they are to you. Believe me, everything you can find in the streets is available at home—and so much more. If you do this right, you'll both have a lifetime to grow into what you both need.

4. **Threat:** The threat could be another woman or a lack of communication, but in reality the threat is you. The other woman is just being herself--she has no commitment to your wife. Don't say things to her that you feel you couldn't say to your wife, and don't ask for her advice about your wife. Not only is this behavior unfair, but it can also lead to playing with fire. Find a trusted male friend, a reputable counselor or spiritual leader to help discuss your concerns so that you will not have the resentment build up and to allow you to get to the place where your wife can become your best friend. Remember at all times that

she is your closest companion. Be true to your commitment to God and your wife--because you have only one time to be unfaithful, which means a single act of unfaithfulness can never be undone.

TAKE AWAY'S

1. If you were attracted to a certain type of woman before marriage, you'll still be attracted after marriage.

2. It's your choice to be faithful or unfaithful.

3. Do a self-examination.

4. Take the exit off the highway of unfaithfulness.

5. When in doubt, JUST SAY NO!

SCRIPTURE READINGS

1. Marriage is honorable in all, and the bed undefiled: but whoremongers and adulterers God will judge.   *Hebrews 13:4*

2. For this is the will of God, even your sanctification, that ye should abstain from fornication. *1 Thessalonians 4:3*

3. Blessed is the man that endureth temptation: for when he is tried, he shall receive the crown of life, which the Lord hath promised to them that love him.   *James 1:12*

4. For in that he himself hath suffered being tempted, he is able to succour them that are tempted.   *Hebrews 2:18*

5. Who can find a virtuous woman? For her price is far above rubies. *Proverbs 3:10*

CHAPTER 7

IT'S ALL IN THE DETAILS

Have you ever wondered why it takes your wife an eternity to run in a store and pick out a birthday card for a friend, when you can get in and out of the store before the door swings shut?

Your wife has to make sure the card says exactly what she wants it to say. On the other hand, you're happy if it's a card with a few kind words. The reason for this difference: In most cases, men are the big dreamers, and we want to do things quickly and on a large scale to reach our dreams. We're focused on the things to come, not the mundane thoughts of today. Most women, however, find joy in making sure they've covered all the details.

Your wife might be more impressed by the smaller things than the larger, or maybe the more sporadic things. The smaller things always add up to be worth more in the long run. If you're looking for small, simple ways to please your wife, use these examples to get started. Every woman is different, so choose wisely.

1. Say good morning every morning with a smile and stop waking up angry.

2. Give your wife a hug and a kiss every morning, but be sure to brush first.

3. Tell your wife every morning that you love and appreciate her.

4. Let your wife see you reading the Bible and praying. Show that you're getting your direction from God.

5. Make the bed if you're the last one to get out of it.

6. Make breakfast from time to time, and sometimes even bring it to her while she's in bed.

7. Take interest in her. For instance, ask about her plans for the day.

8. Be first every day to complement her on her looks and more.

9. Take time out of your day just to call your wife to see how her day is going.

10. If you're the last to leave the house, send her off with a kiss and encourage her to have a great day.

11. If you get home first, welcome her with a kiss and a greeting.

12. Ask about her day and be sure to listen.

13. When she's been gone don't forget to greet her with a hug and kiss, and let her know that you missed her and love her.

14. It's OK to clean up the house--trust me, she won't get mad.

15. Try to do laundry and prepare dinner from time to time, even if you have to order out or hire a cleaning service.

16. Keep her car clean and running.

17. Remember dates and keep them special even if you have to write them in your journal.

18. Establish a date night so you can dress up and go all out to make her fall in love with you all over again.

19. Take pictures so that you can share the years and memories together.

20. Try to know what she wants without your having to ask. Depend on your listening and your journal.

21. Stay in shape and make yourself as attractive as possible. Make her feel that she has a prize, not a punishment.

22. Keep her on her toes. Pick random days to celebrate her.

23. Hold her when you're watching TV together.

24. Read to her.

25. Pray with her.

26. Prepare a bath for her from time to time.

27. Massage her when she's sore.

28. Allow her time to get away (especially if you have children).

29. Always be her friend.

30. Support her in the things she wants to accomplish.

31. Love her family.

32. Always speak in love, even when you're angry.

33. Kiss her and say, "I love you" every night before bed and say good night.

Sit down and make your own list of things you want to do for your wife. She deserves it--and if you don't, someone else will try.

TAKE AWAY'S

1. The game is always won in the trenches, and in the trenches the small things matter.

2. Love your wife—don't try to buy her with expensive items.

3. Remember, most women are detail-oriented. It's amazing what they see and remember.

4. Don't try to change your wife.

5. Open up to allow your wife to become or remain your help meet.

_TO DO's_

1. Start doing small acts of love for your wife _NOW!!_

2. Let your voice of love be heard in the morning before her day begins and at night before she goes to sleep.

3. Put substance to your love through acts of love.

4. Use her strengths to bring you closer together.

5. Do these things because you love her and not for the response. If you do them for the response, you're doing them for the wrong reason.

SCRIPTURE READINGS

1. Enjoy life with your wife, whom you love, all the days of this meaningless life that God has given you under the sun--all your meaningless days. For this is your lot in life and in your toilsome labor under the sun. *Ecclesiastes 9:9*

2. Husbands love your wives, just as Christ loved the church and gave himself up for her. *Ephesians 5:25*

3. In this same way, husbands ought to love their wives as their own bodies. He who loves his wife loves himself. *Ephesians 5:28*

4. Love never fails. But where there are prophecies, they will cease; where there are tongues, they will be stilled; where there is knowledge, it will pass away. For we know in part and we prophesy in part, but when perfection comes imperfection disappears. *1 Corinthians 13: 8-10*

5. In all thy ways acknowledge him, and he shall direct thy paths.   *Proverbs 3:6*

CHAPTER 8
HAVE FUN

A good marriage must have a foundation of friendship. Your wife won't always have a perfect body, and your Mister Universe days are numbered, so build your marriage on something you can always fall back on.

When was the last time you laughed with your wife or spent some time being silly together? The ability to have fun together will get you through the tough times. But first you must know what your wife likes to do, and she must know what you like to do. Also make sure you enjoy some activities that don't cost money, because fun shouldn't always have a monetary value attached to it. Be playful with one another. Consider playing harmless jokes on each other. Make it your duty to bring a smile or laugh to your spouse's face once a day. If your wife hasn't laughed since the mid '80s, just go for the smile--the laugh will follow later.

Participate in activities that you both enjoy and that spark conversation between you and your wife. One person shouldn't be having fun while the other is looking at the activity as a necessary evil. Consider this checklist when looking for ways to have fun with your spouse:

1. Are you both truly having fun?

2. Are you growing closer together because of the activity you're doing together?

3. Does time seem to fly by when you're together or does it seem to drag?

4. Is your wife genuinely smiling and showing affection or is she faking it?

5. Do you both look forward to the next outing?

If you catch yourself saying, "This is going to be fun and you'd better like it," trust me, she's not having fun.

Relationships come and go but a true friendship last a lifetime. To build a strong marriage, keep these cornerstones in mind:

1. Make God the head of your marriage.

2. Allow your foundation to be the friendship in your marriage.

3. Let your love be the driving force for your actions.

4. Remember love is a choice. Choose to have a great marriage.

TAKE AWAY'S

1. Your wife must be your best friend.

2. Let God be the head of your marriage, and make friendship the foundation.

3. Laughter prolongs life.

4. Make sure the fun is mutual.

5. Speak positively when referring to your wife.

_TO DO's_

1. Make a list of things that you like doing.

2. Make a list of things your wife enjoys doing.

3. Compare the two lists and choose a few activities you both enjoy.

4. Evaluate to see if you both are having fun.

5. Keep your activities fresh and exciting.

SCRIPTURE READINGS

1. For ye shall go out with joy, and be led forth with peace: the mountains and the hills shall break forth before you into singing, and all the trees of the field shall clap their hands.
    Isaiah 55:12

2. For our heart shall rejoice in Him, because we have trusted in His holy name. *Psalm 33:21*

3. Thou hast put gladness in my heart, more than in the time that their corn and wine increased.
    Psalm 4:7

4. Casting all your care upon him; for he careth for you.   *1 Peter 5:7*

5. Therefore take no thought, saying, What shall we eat? or, What shall we drink? or, Wherewithal shall we be clothed? (For after all these things do the Gentiles seek:) for your heavenly Father knoweth that ye have need of all things.   *Matthew 6:31-32*

CHAPTER 9

HAVE A LIFE
AND
KEEP IT YOURS

When you reviewed the list you made after reading the previous chapter, did you notice there are some things you like to do that your wife doesn't quite care for--and vice-versa? You may enjoy working on cars or playing golf, for example, while she may enjoy Pilates or arts and crafts. You may enjoy ESPN; she may like the Oxygen channel.

Don't force your spouse to take part in these activities. Instead, consider these as your very own hobbies or interests and enjoy them on your own time. Here's how to enjoy your free time without getting into trouble.

First, and I can't express this enough, if you're not participating in a hobby or interest by yourself, make sure you're in the presence of men who have integrity and can keep you accountable. During this time in fellowship, keep your mouth shut about how terrible your wife is, or how she won't do--or always does--certain things that pluck that last nerve, you know the one, the one that prevents you from become the "Incredible Hulk" . The purpose of this activity isn't to slander your wife. It's OK to seek wise counsel, but never speak ill of your wife. (If you happen to be a wife reading this book, this applies to you, too. Women, find godly women who can keep you accountable, and make sure they're married or have an idea of what a strong marriage looks like. It's always wise to check the source of your advice.)

Make sure you have a hobby, not something you do just when you're angry. Otherwise, this activity becomes a hiding place, not something you do to grow individually. It should be something you do when you just need to get away or give her time away from you. Yes, she might need some time away from you. She might not always think you're God's gift to women.

Here are some other points to think about when dealing with your small piece of serenity:

1. Never, ever let your wife feel that she's secondary to your hobbies. Think carefully about how you present your ideas when you're looking to spend time away from your wife.

2. Never rush your time with your wife so that you can hurry and get to your favorite activity. You might need to start your bonding time earlier, for example, so you can keep your tee time. It's not good to leave a wife at home when she wants to spend that time with you. Your efforts might backfire.

3. Never put your wife off when you see she wants to spend time with you. Now, if your cell phone was off while you were playing cards or golfing, it's just good manners to finish the game and call her afterward. But if you take the call, you must be committed to it.

4. A good leader knows how to avoid unnecessary confrontations. So never pit your wife against your hobby.

5. Keep a mental log of how much time you're spending away from wife and family and make sure you're not the absent husband. A lonely spouse can lead to lots of problems. Also if

you have children, be sure to divide the time up so that you both can experience some time to unwind.

6. Make sure your activities suit a married man. That's right, no online dating.

7. It's OK to discuss what you're doing with your spouse, because you want to avoid the appearance of subterfuge at all times. Remember, you're not hiding anything-- you're just doing something you enjoy without your spouse. Never put her trust in you in jeopardy.

8. **CAUTION:** Men; never let another man have his way around your home when you're not there. If you are to have a rendezvous meet in public.

9. Don't turn your home into the local hangout. Your priorities lie with God and your family first. Plus, this might put your wife into an unfair or compromising situation. There's a reason the Bible says the flesh is weak. So protect yourself.

10. Think like a married man regardless of whom you're with or where you are. Character is what you do when no one else is watching.

Above all, make sure your hobbies add to your marriage rather than take something away from it. Life goes by quicker than you know, so enjoy your spouse and enjoy yourself.

TAKE AWAY'S

1. Have a hobby.

2. Don't hide it from your wife.

3. After God, keep your wife first.

4. Schedule your outings in advance.

5. Think like a married man.

TO DO's

1. Plan time apart from your wife.

2. Always keep her feelings first.

3. Never talk badly about your wife.

4. Check the source of your advice.

5. Don't turn your hobby into a hiding place.

SCRIPTURE READINGS

1. The LORD is with you, while ye be with Him; and if ye seek Him, He will be found of you; but if ye forsake Him, He will forsake you.
    2 Chronicles 15:2

2. Sow to yourself in righteousness, reap in mercy; break up your fallow ground: for it is time to seek the LORD, till He come and rain righteousness upon you.   *Hosea 10:12*

3. But without faith it is impossible to please Him: for he that cometh to God must believe that He is, and that He is a rewarder of them that diligently seek him.   *Hebrews 11:6*

4. The LORD is good unto them that wait for Him, to the soul that seeketh Him.
    Lamentations 3:25

5. But seek first His kingdom and His righteousness, and all these things will be given to you as well.   *Matthew 6:33*

HHH

CHAPTER 10

SEX IS NOT A WEAPON

How many times has your wife come to bed in her defensive gear? You know the outfit--the one that makes her look as though she's going camping or on a safari? Do you remember the time you woke up in the middle of the night and couldn't go back to sleep, so you thought it was a sign from God to make love? When you woke her up, however, she wasn't that agreeable, and you didn't understand why. Do you feel that as long as she has a pulse, you can work with the rest? If you do, welcome to the club of a lot of husbands.

For most women, the whole idea of making love is more mental than physical. As men, we love the physical part of love. We enjoy the touching and feeling, we enjoy the whole sensual experience with our wives. For her, on the other hand, talking and holding are very important. Further, feeling special and being catered to mean just as much as the physical act.

For this reason--and many others--sex is one of the most controversial and misunderstood parts of marriage. For instance, the Bible states that your wife's body belong to you and your body belongs to her, and she can't say no anymore unless you're in agreement, and vice-versa (see 1 Corinthians 7:3-5). But don't get too happy and be a fool. This doesn't mean that you go and take what is yours and disrespect your wife and her feelings. No means no. This passage really means that neither of you should use sex as a weapon.

Consider the old if - then statement: If you do this for me then we can do that, or vice-versa. Normally this doesn't work for guys anyway, but some women use it against us. Let's face it: Most of the time we cave in under pressure because we can't hold out for long. Also remember that women are not the only ones who play games. If you are trying to be a master gamer stop and be honest with the one you want to be honest with you, it will help the relationship in the long run.

If you want to keep your love life healthy and avoid these games, you must know your wife. More times than not, a woman will know that morning if she wants to make love that day or not, and it's your job to pick up on the signs she sends your way. She might actually want to participate more often than you think, but all women are different. Pay attention and watch for these possible clues:

1. What type of underwear did she put on this morning—sexy or nonsexy? (Use her standards, not yours.)

2. Did she spend extra time this morning making herself more appealing to you?

3. Is she trying something new?

4. Do a time-of-the-month check. (Know your wife).

5. Is she overly affectionate today?

6. Is she leaving verbal clues?

7. Look around and check the ambiance.

8. Is she wearing makeup or perfume when she normally doesn't?

9. What is she wearing to bed?

A wife can throw many clues your way--it all comes back to knowing your wife. Now, just because she might be giving you one or more clues doesn't mean that you're home free. Your job, if you accept the mission, is to appeal to her mental needs. More times than not, our wives want the same things we do, but we mess it up. How? Because I can't name all the ways, I'll give you some of the duties we must keep in mind if we want to be successful.

1. Continue to make her feel special and loved.

2. Don't let her tire herself out.

3. Don't argue with her.

4. Have soft conversations (Talk, listen).

5. Make sure you're cleaned and groomed.

6. Be sexy. Please keep yourself in shape.

7. Don't be too aggressive. Move slowly, until the time is right.

8. Take care of the kids and send them to bed.

9. Leave hints as well.

10. Always make it special. Don't approach this special time as though you're having the oil changed in the car.

11. Never ask about your performance. Trust me, you know.

12. Always leave a satisfied wife. You want and need her repeat business.

13. Focus on your love, not just the physical act. This whole process is approximately 85 percent mental, 10 percent physical and 5 percent timing.

Once you start picking up on your wife's hints and listening to her expressed needs, you'll enjoy more moments of pleasure, both planned and spontaneous. If you make love to her mind, the body will follow, and that combination will take you to levels you didn't think were possible with your wife.

TAKE AWAY'S

1. Don't use sex as a weapon.

2. Make love to her mind and the body will follow.

3. Pay attention to your wife.

4. Don't rush her--slow and easy works better.

5. Keep her guessing.

TO DO's

1. Listen to your wife's needs.

2. Work your personal checklist.

3. Let her know you want her the way she wants to be had.

4. Have a date night.

5. Do your job (make her a loyal client who loves to come back for repeat business).

SCRIPTURE READINGS

1. The husband should fulfill his marital duty to his wife, and likewise the wife to her husband. *1 Corinthians 7:3*

2. The wife's body does not belong to her alone but also to her husband. In the same way, the husband's body does not belong to him alone but also to his wife. *1 Corinthians 7:4*

3. Do not deprive each other except by mutual consent and for a time, so that you may devote yourself to prayer. Then come together again so that Satan will not tempt you because of your lack of self-control. *1 Corinthians 7:5*

4. For this cause shall a man leave his father and mother, and shall be joined unto his wife, and they two shall be one flesh. *Ephesians 5:31*

5. My soul shall be satisfied as with marrow and fatness; and my mouth shall praise thee with joyful lips. *Psalm 63:5*

6. Read all eight chapters of the Song of Solomon to get a true understanding of passion and how to implement in your life.

FINAL TAKE AWAY'S

HHH

1. Keep God the head of your house and life.

2. Remember you and your wife are different.

3. Don't engage.

4. Listen

5. You're a leader, not a dictator

6. Keep friendship the foundation of your marriage.

7. Choose love every day.

8. Just say no to temptation.

9. Check the source of your advice.

10. Don't invite other men into your home.

11. Sex is not a weapon.

12. Commit for life.

FINAL TO DO's

HHH

1. Read your Bible daily.

2. Read this book as many times as needed.

3. Start a journal.

4. No man is an island. Find other married male friends of integrity to keep you accountable.

5. Find a church home and allow God to lead you.

6. Pray continuously.

7. Choose your battles.

8. Be affectionate to your wife.

9. Allow your wife the opportunity to be your help meet.

10. Keep track of your progress.

11. Set personal goals.

12. When you finish reading this, hug and kiss your wife and let her know you love her.

So in conclusion, always remember that you are in this marriage for the long haul and a Happy Husband begins with a Happy Wife. Also, remember that the only person that can control you; is you, so keep that in mind the next time you feel like saying you make me sick, or something negative in the way she so called influenced you.

This book is not written to be the say all and be all, but it is written to make you think and allow you to focus on what is important in your relationship. Because everyman's marriage is not every man's marriage, which means every man marriage is different and require different amounts of attention. So my last bit of advice will be, Love your wife and enjoy your life.

About the Author

Sly Fleming , a resident of Bowie, Maryland, has been an example of the saying, "It takes a village to raise a child." He reminds us that if we stand tall, it is because we stand on the shoulders of others. Growing up in a small community in North Carolina where GOD, family, education, and hard work were stressed, he had many positive influences in his life.

Sly received his BS in electrical engineering from North Carolina A&T State University and his MBA from Averett University . He spreads the ministry of Jesus Christ through public speaking, providing financial advice, being involved in drama ministries, and singing in his church's praise and worship ministries. He's also a local MC and comic when called upon. But Sly most enjoys fellowshipping with others, especially his family, which includes his wife and two sons.

Sly Fleming, is also the author of "*30 Days of Love, A Spiritual Journey*" and has appeared on several relationship shows such as *The Audrey Chapman Show* and *The Celestial Break* by Marsha Summers. Sly Fleming has encountered and counseled many different couples on staying together and being able to focus on certain areas of their relationship. He is also a business owner and well sought after speaker in many different topics. Sly Fleming has appeared on local TV shows as an actor, in programs such as *The Straight and the Narrow* and held a leading role in plays such as *The Christmas Wish* by **R.A.W Entertainment**. Sly Fleming is the CEO of **Fleming Enterprises and Services Inc. (www.fleminges.com)** and the founder of **The Omukisa**

Foundation also known as *The Second Chance Ministries*, which prides itself on giving back to those that are less fortunate. Not only is Sly Fleming a performer and a business man, but he is an activist standing up for what is right when few will stand (www.ubsfsdiscrimination.com). Sly Fleming has been successful for some of the best in corporate America and for himself: however, he believes his greatest accomplishments are; being a Happy Husband and father of two. In his own words, he is just an ordinary man looking for extraordinary results.

www.ingramcontent.com/pod-product-compliance
Lightning Source LLC
Chambersburg PA
CBHW031247280526
45784CB00004B/1749